A Girl Named Entropy

Jaime A. Contrys

Presentation by *BookLeaf Publishing*

Web: www.bookleafpub.com

E-mail: info@bookleafpub.com

ISBN: 9789357441803

First edition 2023

To those born in muddy water,

may you never stop seeking the light.

ACKNOWLEDGEMENT

Thank you to all of those who believed in me and encouraged me. You know who you are. I love you. Thank you to Bookleaf Publishing for this amazing opportunity.

Chamomile and Ketamine

I never thought people actually went insane.
Tip-toeing on the edge of that abyss,
every day I walk amongst regular folk,
trying to live their lives with their cars,
phones and credit scores.
They don't see that I'm a hair-trigger away
from burning this world to cinders.

I didn't think people really went insane.
But God and the demons arrived as
snow drifted high on the garbage piled
in the street, and they kept you occupied while
robbing me of the shreds of hope I clung to.

He wasn't you—
that man who held me
in bed as he spoke of underworlds
and cacodemon contracts, and — oh god,
I didn't want him to touch me.
Didn't want anyone to.
Though at least, it was quiet then.

You were jumping off the subway platform as
I smoked out of the bathroom window
of our four-story walk up.
Even then,
the voices took you
for days, weeks,
eternity, I think.

Let's be honest, mi amor,
our descent into madness started
long before the snow started to melt.
Or the warm days spent
lounging in the breathless
blue of the Caribbean.

God was speaking to you,
through you,
and I didn't want to be the
queen of hell, baby.
I just wanted to sleep again.

Refraction

You were the sunlight that broke
through the ocean's surface;
Illuminating the dark water,
pushing my fears to the
depths of the sandy floor.

Evening Lament

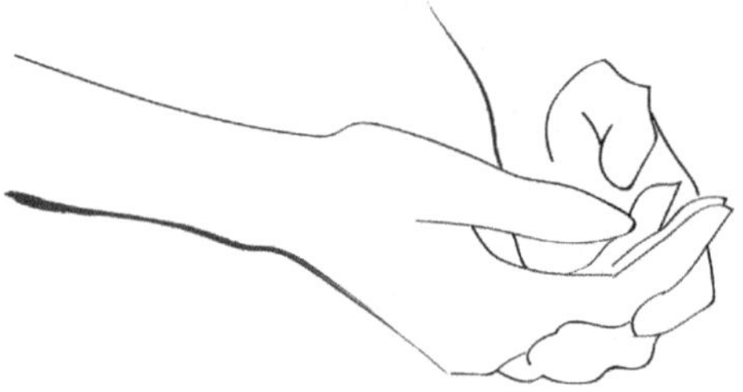

Old earl grey tea bags still
stain the countertop from the
last time you were here.

Dried red roses sit in a vase ringed
with demarcation lines of water long
evaporated while fallen petals
crumble around them.

Stale cigarette smoke clings
to every surface as empty pill bottles
clutter the cabinet, and the only
food in the fridge is wilted
lettuce in the bottom drawer.

If you were here, you would tell me,
"You need to take better care of yourself."
But

you're not,

and I

won't.

January Mourning

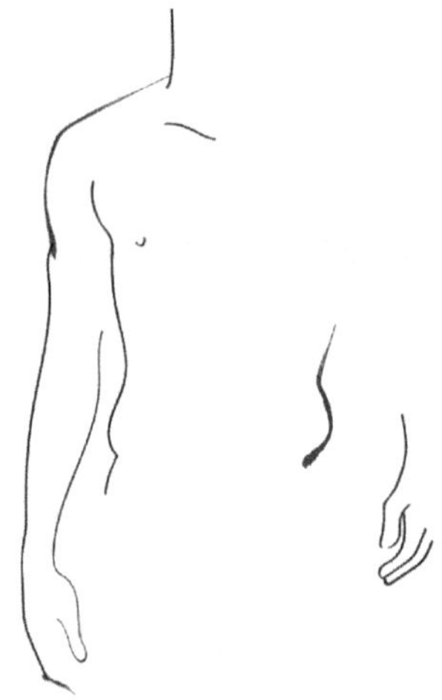

The window is cracked
as rain dribbles outside
and I grumble at the gray
clouds that cast an
ugly hue over the
entire city.

I wish I was waking up
on this iced drizzly morning
next to him. Naked
limbs intertwined
as our hearts beat fast,
and our lips move
slow.

March 19th

One day we will meet again.
Sweat will trickle down
our spines, glinting in
the noonday light.
Or a cool breeze will wake us
to the lazy tide lapping
the sand at our feet.

We will find each other again,
and our honeysuckle love
at the brink of an eternal paradise.

We, two children of the sea,
will dance under the milky
moonlight for the rest
of whatever's left.

Wait for me there, my darling,
in the dojo under the sun.

Summer Regrets

July afternoon sun beats down on my skin,
as the heat ripples over the concrete
in iridescent waves while I cover
my eyes with the crook of my elbow.

Sweat pools in between my breasts and
it's getting harder to breathe with every
passing second. I can't help but think of the days
spent bustling through the train,
the clinking of glasses, talking passengers,
or swearing in the kitchen before sneaking a
swig of wine from the bottle.

I wish I would have told you how I felt then.
How you felt like sinking into a warm bath
after a long cold day, or how laughing with you
made my cheeks hurt from smiling—
Oh god, most of all,
how that still haunts me.

Does the sun burn my flesh or is it the memories
of your arms around my waist?
Is it the unforgiving heat that dries my throat,
or the idea that I let you
slip through my fingers?

Time Traveler

People leave in one form or another.
You can even leave yourself,
as I have done, since before I could count.
I can leave my body and float to the sky,
the stars, to small islands that breathe out
magic as the brine of cerulean waves
lull you to sleep on gemstone beaches.
But empty bodies have a hard time
staying upright when there's
nothing anchoring them to the world.

You never understood why I
let them touch me, taste me,
fill every bit of me that was hollow
and aching. I was not me,
and they were not them as
we delighted in the torture of
being so wrong for each other it felt
like it was the odds-defying kind of right.
Yet, it's always me crumbled
on the bathroom floor at 3 AM.

Love gets lost in the turbines of life,
or the voices in their head have them
taken to padded cells in handcuffs.
Your best friends stop answering
the phone to send messages saying
that you broke their hearts when
you were just trying to find
the
        will
            to
                survive.

Sweet, They Called Me

Twice have I lived in corner basement rooms
with boxes of food storage piled to the
ceiling as make-shift walls.
Cold rooms make colder hands
and old aches resurface as I let in strays
to stave off the hunger pressing in.

I never voiced aloud that growing up alone
put an irreparable silence behind the
floodgates of my mind.
Instead of a gilded youth-hood,

in my beginning, I was dawned with
an echo of ice in my veins to
manifest as a shield of rage.

My hands bled and cracked as
the cardboard boxes were shredded
and cans of beans spilled in the chaos
of finding myself amongst the rubble of
emotional absence.

What goes unsaid is this:
Hell isn't a place in the afterlife.
It's something we haul around with us,
as our parents did.

As their parents did.

Spring Ting

We smoked, drank, and
your toffee eyes brushed over my
skin as a midday summer sun.
Under the covers we found paradise,
I could hear the waves in your chest,
and taste the brine on your lips.
I crawled onto your bed
and made a home there.
I swear when we woke,
there was sand in our hair.

Dominican Hurricane

I left the doors open as it started to pour.
It ripped the wallpaper down in ribbons
and broke the furniture to splinters.
Shattered stained-glass windows,
and flooded the basement
before it even asked to come in.

I don't remember now,
why I let it rage on for so long,
but can I still feel the rain on my face.
White Hennessy and menthols and
the sweetness of making love on the
beach of Jaragua National park,

how I loved the storm of you.

Two Paths

Teeth and skin and blood,
claws scraping my spine at twilight.
I was born in a full moon hurricane,
so when the soft spring rain came,
I only heard the thunder clapping.

You felt like the storms that would
knock over trees,
tear down power lines, and
have us lighting candles to see
as the sun fell behind the red mountains.

The house would rattle and groan,
and my body tingled with the cocktail
of excitement and fear thrumming
through my veins.

You were fire and war and howling at the
blood-torn sky and he —
He was sparkling morning dew on
vermillion blades of grass,
stolen glances,
and grazing fingertips.
He was longing
and wishing on stars
and whispered prayers
in the nightscape.

He was sore cheeks from endless laughter
and moonlight kisses at the stream
in the flickering light of the bonfire.

While you were raw throats and nails
digging into flesh, sobbing and madness—
Years of nightmares and cold sweats,
and waking in the sweltering black
to the flashback of you fucking her
in the other room.

Though, there are some hope-tinged dreams
of what could have been
that leave Forget-Me-Not
stains on the pillowcases, and
murmur to the beat of my resting heart,

"I remember, I remember, I remember."

Atrophy

~You come in late,
the street lamp flickers from snow falling.
Discarding your clothes at the end of the bed,
cold hands pull down the covers as
my naked body tightens at the exposure.
Your lips find my skin, throat, shoulder.
You taste like menthols and Mexican beer.
I encase you in my limbs, my everything.~

I started leaving the door unlocked,
hoping someone,

anyone,
would wander into the apartment
and take me from my fever dreams.

You did so once upon a time,
when I'd write poems on your whiteboard,
and leave notes taped to the apartment
door as I slept in red lace lingerie,
waiting for you to come home to me.

Where Three Deserts Meet

When I was born, a fine coat of red
sand settled on my skin,
and my hair grew out like wild sage.

My mother taught me how to crawl
as the lizards do, in between the cacti
so birds of prey won't spot me.

From my father, I learned how to blend
into the landscapes, and sound out my warnings
as the Great Basin rattlesnake.

Grandmother moon reached down
with her borrowed light, and encouraged
howls from my yellow-eyed coyote siblings.

These freckles on my shoulders were earned
from afternoons spent walking about dried
river beds as the noble tarantulas do.

My homeland is a place where,
in less than a day the summer sun can kill the
mightiest of men, and
water is more precious than gold.

The Musing

I'm in the bar where lights flash rainbows
as drinks spill on the dance floor,
but I'm thinking about
Achilles grieving Patroclus.
Dragging Hector around the outskirts
of Troy with his battle cry ringing through the
air.

Sometimes it's not about love nor lust,
It's about pure connection.
Touch without worry.
Fingertips brushing the back of a neck,
grazing the hairline.
Whisper for the moment,
at least, in this,
you're safe with me.

No wonder the demi-god went mad.
I would have burned the city,
no, the *world*,
to the ground
for you.

Santo Domingo, September '19

The wet heat never seems to end,
and the mango tree out front
provides little shade.
Abuela cooks rice and beans
for lunch, and he and I will take
 a walk to the corner bodega.

We'll wander through
the Colonial Zone
until the sun bakes me

to a living crisp,
and we'll find shelter
in a new bar where
chilled Presidente fogs
our glasses and
we clink to the good life.

Heartache Photosynthesis

Oxygen enters my lungs,
and carbon dioxide exits.
If it's that simple,
maybe the love I still carry
for you will be exhaled,
as will the taste of your skin,
the sound of your laugh,
and the amber of your sleepy eyes
first thing in the morning.

Twenty Fourteen

Days tick past,
slow,
Eyes burning,
red,
body shivering,
cold showers and
gasping,
trying to get through
the day without vomiting
so hard I bleed.

Vodka has more value
than anything else I've
yet mustered up the
courage to face, and the
the safest way to escape
the memories of your fingers
bruising my hip bones, or
your teeth scraping down
my neck is by crawling into
the beds of those
not important to me.

They don't care if
they leave marks,
and I don't want to kiss
after making them come.
I only hope that the year will pass,
and my mind will not be so full
with thoughts of
you.

desert lotus

Light stains the pale walls creamy white as
a breeze ruffles the leaves of the cotton tree
outside my window,

and the sun is greeted by sparse puffy clouds.
A passing orange tabby stops to
peer at me in the morning glow.

A pause, a look shared between consciousness,
and my fingers graze the cool glass.
I could have sworn I saw a twitch in the
little creamsicle paw.

Without realizing it, a spark
had split through the muddy water,
and joy began to sprout as I found myself
home at last.

Mosaic

Green sea glass and purple olive shells,
dirty black and white checkered floors,
and crown moulded hells decorate the inside
of the museum in which I dwell.

Iridescent light shines through stained windows,
and the good china is still speckled with
vermilion
paint from many addled suppers spent with
bottles
of sweet wine and a decrepit copy of "Ariel."

Half-finished murals of fine-sanded beaches,
glittering fireworks over the isthmus
and a still life of his favorite sweater he gave
away at the bar the night you left without
saying goodbye.

These old bones carry the colors of eyes,
locks of hair, and hold impressions of bodies
felt from those past lives everyone talks about.

It takes centuries to realize
 we're all starving artists
hoping someone, anyone,
perhaps even ourselves,
will stop to admire our art after
we chop off our ears and
mourn what used to be.

Interstellar

I thought I was born with a
hole inside my chest.
There were ashen white roses
tied with black ribbons at
the grave of early loss.
I poured myself into those
I loved with shreds of tattered
hope, pleading with stars that
they'd find a reason to stay.

Seeking truth, I tracked down God
and found a neon "CLOSED" sign.
I fought the mystics and the spirits,
and wound myself up in a wooden
horse to face my Trojans
and their thieving princes.

Here's what I discovered in the blunders:
it wasn't a black hole threatening
to consume me for eternity.

At my center, I found everything.
I hold the universe,
as she holds me.

Eyes: loved and lost

warm amber flecked with swirling gold
cinnamon speckled honey whiskey
stormy seas and monstera leaves
dark roasted coffee and wrought iron
pale morning cornflower and
silver-lined hope